AF228577

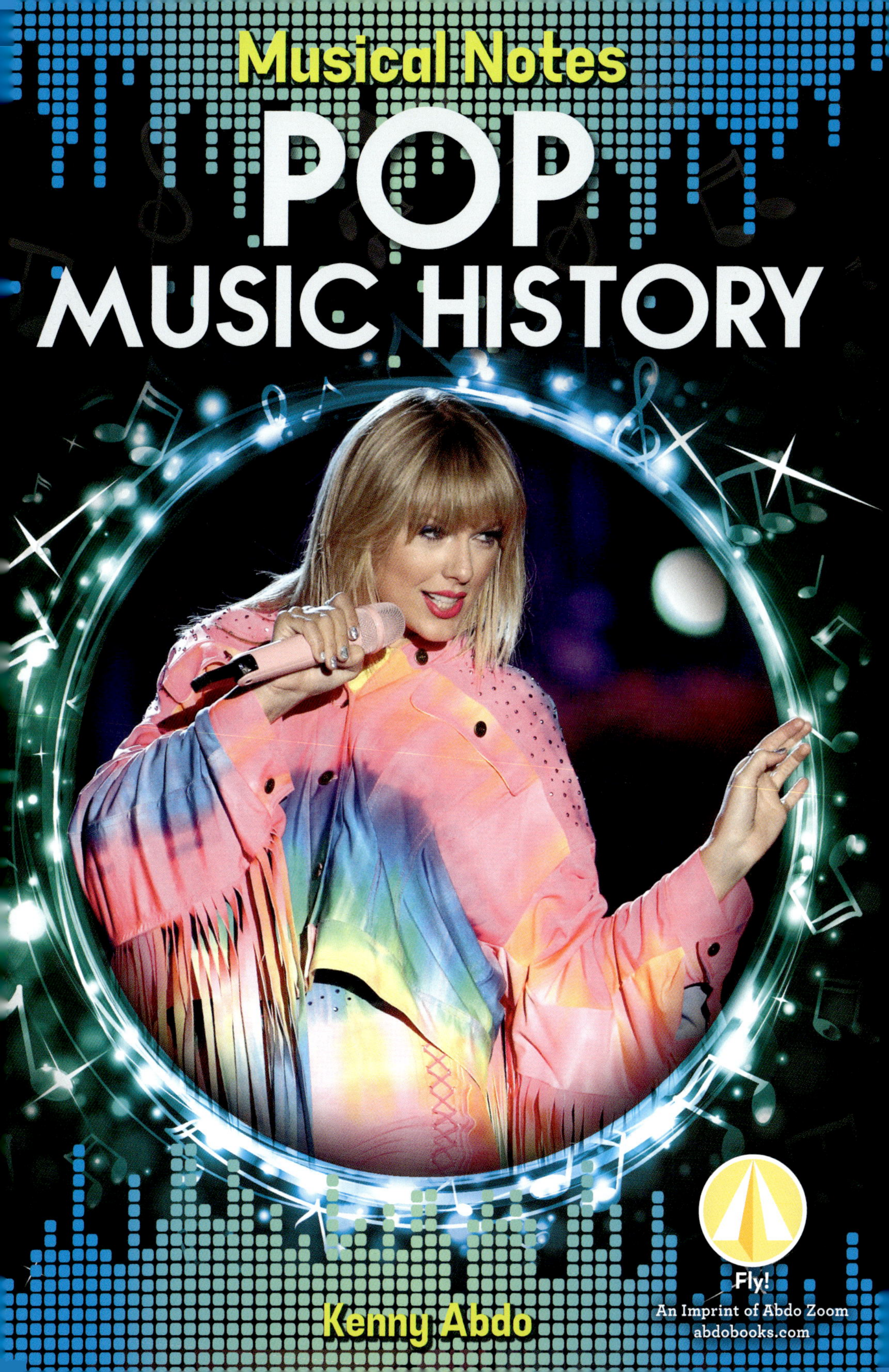

Musical Notes
POP MUSIC HISTORY
Fly!
An Imprint of Abdo Zoom
abdobooks.com
Kenny Abdo

abdobooks.com

Published by Abdo Zoom, a division of ABDO, P.O. Box 398166, Minneapolis, Minnesota 55439. Copyright © 2020 by Abdo Consulting Group, Inc. International copyrights reserved in all countries. No part of this book may be reproduced in any form without written permission from the publisher. Fly!™ is a trademark and logo of Abdo Zoom.

Printed in the United States of America, North Mankato, Minnesota.
102019
012020

Photo Credits: Alamy, Getty Images, Shutterstock
Production Contributors: Kenny Abdo, Jennie Forsberg, Grace Hansen
Design Contributors: Dorothy Toth, Neil Klinepier

Library of Congress Control Number: 2019941324

Publisher's Cataloging-in-Publication Data

Names: Abdo, Kenny, author.
Title: Pop music history / by Kenny Abdo
Description: Minneapolis, Minnesota : Abdo Zoom, 2020 | Series: Musical notes | Includes online resources and index.
Identifiers: ISBN 9781532129438 (lib. bdg.) | ISBN 9781098220419 (ebook) | ISBN 9781098220907 (Read-to-Me ebook)
Subjects: LCSH: Popular music--Juvenile literature. | Music and history--Juvenile literature. | Music, Popular (Songs, etc.)--Juvenile literature. | Alternative pop/rock music--Juvenile literature. | Techno-pop (Music)--Juvenile literature.
Classification: DDC 782.42164--dc23

TABLE OF CONTENTS

POP MUSIC

Lighting up the **charts**, pop music has defined each decade with a unique sound that blares through speakers around the world!

Pop music used to describe whatever was popular at the time. Today, it has grown into a **genre** of its own that changes with its audience.

OPENING
ACT

Music **producer** Mitch Miller worked with the trendiest musicians of the 1950s. He was known for his creative ways to get new sounds out of artists.

Johnny Mathis, Aretha Franklin, and others became stars because of Miller's methods. Pop music grew into an upbeat sound that was especially aimed at teens.

HEADLINER

During the 60s, the sounds of The Beach Boys, The Supremes, and Ray Charles filled the airwaves with their **melodic** and cheerful tunes!

Pop began to mix with other **genres** starting in the 70s. The most famous being pop-rock. Elton John, David Bowie, and The Jackson 5 became worldwide **icons** with their catchy songs.

The 80s changed pop music **culture**. On **MTV**, Prince combined rock and funk to make a sound all his own. Tiffany performed for teens around the country at shopping malls.

The 90s saw rise of the pop group. Boy bands like N'Sync danced and sang their way into mega-fame. The Spice Girls' song "Wannabe" remains the best selling single by any female group in history.

Today, pop music is as rich and influential as ever. Taylor Swift went from country music superstar to the queen of pop. The 10-time Grammy Award winner received the Teen Choice Awards' first ever **Icon** Award in 2019.

TEEN
CHOICE
2019
ICON AWARD
TAYLOR
SWIFT

GLOSSARY

chart – a list that shows which music has sold the most during a period of time.

culture – the customs, arts, language, and more of a nation or a group of people.

genre – a type of art, music, or literature.

icon – a celebrity whose fame and popularity stays the same or increases through time.

melody – an arrangement of musical notes that creates a song.

Music Television (MTV) – an international cable television channel that debuted in 1981. It was a first of its kind to play new and popular music videos around the clock.

producer – a person who manages the recording and production of a music album.

single – an individual song from a full album released as a promotion.

ONLINE RESOURCES

To learn more about pop music history, please visit **abdobooklinks.com** or scan this QR code. These links are routinely monitored and updated to provide the most current information available.

INDEX